ABOVE SAN FRANCISCO

by ROBERT CAMERON

A new collection of nostalgic and contemporary
aerial photographs of the Bay Area

with text by
HERB CAEN

Cameron and Company, San Francisco, California

TABLE OF CONTENTS

Such a book as this does not reach publication without more than the usual amount of cooperation from many people. So, for their encouragement and expertise, I thank the following:

Douglas Brookes, Robert Burger, Todd Cameron, Ken Cellini, Mayor Dianne Feinstein, William Ganslen, Victor Gonzales, Frederick Gorell, John Goy, Gladys Hansen, Alice Harth, Charlotte Mailliard, Robert Maldonado, Mary Martinet, Ken McNeil, Jr., Kent Munson, Patricia O'Grady, Dolly Patterson

and especially pilots:
James E. Larsen, James M. Larsen, Ken Suzuki, and Al Wilsey.

Credit For Historical Photographs:
Bancroft Library, Marilyn Blaisdell Collection, Hoover Institution Library, Library of Congress, Mill Valley Public Library, National Archive, Oakland Museum, Pacific Aerial Survey, San Francisco Chronicle, and the San Francisco Public Library.

CAMERON and COMPANY

543 Howard Street   San Francisco, California 94105   415/777-5582   800/779-5582   Fax 415/777-4814

Library of Congress Catalogue number: 86-071483
Above San Francisco ISBN 0-918684-28-5
©1986 by Robert W. Cameron and Company, Inc. All rights reserved.

First Printing, 1986
Second Printing, 1987
Third Printing, 1988
Fourth Printing, 1990
Fifth Printing, 1991
Sixth Printing, 1993

Book design by
JANE OLAUG KRISTIANSEN

Color processing by The New Lab, San Francisco, G.P. Color, Los Angeles, Modern Effects, San Francisco, and Art Form, Los Angeles.
Typography by Parker-Smith Typography, San Francisco and Reeder Type, Fremont, California.
Color Separations and Printing by Dai Nippon Printing Co., Hong Kong.

Of all the great picture-book cities, San Francisco may be the most tantalizing. Now you see it, now you don't – an ever-changing panorama of shifting patterns and drifting fog, the dizzying interplay of light and shadows among the hills that both exalt and obstruct. It is a peek-a-boo, hide-and-seek city, forever elusive, its endless secrets lurking in nameless alleys, hidden gardens and pathways that lead through stately corridors of eucalyptus and then vanish somewhere into the misty Pacific.

It's an odd quality, this pervasive air of mystery, for on the face of it, San Francisco seems the most accessible of world cities. It is so small – about 49 square miles, seven by seven – that I once wrote, in a not uncommon fit of hyperbole, that I could stand on Twin Peaks "and cup the city in my hands." And so it seems from that dramatic vantage point. On the surface, at least, all of San Francisco is visible, from the downtown towers to the shrinking sea; from the flat Mission District, with its church towers and palm trees, to the even flatter Marina, fringed with yachts. The world's most dramatic bridges are there, arching their backs as they spring across the bay.

The thousands of little houses built by the late Henry Doelger march through the Sunset District to Ocean Beach. Golden Gate Park, another man-made creation (all hail, William Hammond Hall and John McLaren), covers a thousand acres of what was once a Sahara of sand dunes; alongside, the Richmond District turns its old bay windows toward the sun, sometimes a vain gesture, for this is the "fog belt." Market Street slashing through the downtown from its launching pad at the venerable Ferry Building (our most beloved landmark), the park-like Presidio green in the distance, the elegance of Nob Hill and Grace Cathedral – these are only a few of the facets of this gem-like city that are immediately visible.

And yet, to pursue the tantalizing theme, San Francisco remains an enigma, for all its apparent openness. For one thing, the past is forever getting in the way, cluttering up the vision and the visionaries. In few young cities (it was founded in 1850) does a short but turbulant history play such an important role. Nostalgia is as much a part of the atmosphere as the pearly fog, painting halos around streetlamps. There is constant tension between those who want the city to remain what it was – the "Little San Franciscans," to whom small is beautiful and old is sacred – and what I call the manic-progressives, who scoff at the yesterdays and think only of building higher and faster. And if a treasured landmark stands in the way, call in the bulldozers.

It is hard not to think of San Francisco in feminine terms, perhaps, because of her curves and undulations and her Barbary Coast reputation as a "naughty" hoyden. This approach rapidly becomes precious and even cloying, I agree, but the image has a certain validity as the opposing forces battle over her fate, as in an old melodrama. The old-timers see themselves as gallantly fighting to save her honor, while the new San Franciscans feel it's time the old crone was rehabilitated with some new jewelry and a dozen 60-story gowns.

Meanwhile, for all her past excesses and present mistakes, she remains intensely attractive, fulfilling the words of the architect Frank Lloyd Wright, who said 40 years ago, before the real depredations began, that "only a city as beautiful as this could survive what you people are doing to it." We must thank nature more than man for this incomparable setting in its own little world of crashing waves, strong tides and brisk breezes forever rippling the banners and whistling between the towers of Baghdad-by-the-Bay.

San Francisco is a challenge. For all its smallness, where is its heart and soul? When a cable car lurches around a corner of Chinatown on a foggy night, we sometimes feel its essence. The view from Coit Tower at night, with mysterious lights moving slowly across a black velvet bay – this too, is a bit of it. Sometimes the soul seems near at hand in North Beach, where the twin towers of Saints Peter and Paul smile down on Washington Square, with its *paisanos* talking of their childhood in far-off Lucca. In the Mission, the soul is Spanish and the *chicanas* dark-eyed and provocative. The heart of San Francisco is easy to find among the skyscrapers of the financial district and the fine stores of the Union Square area, but the soul remains elusive.

Poets, authors, and hacks like myself have been struggling for years to capture and set down the secret of San Francisco – generally failing. The poet laureate, George Sterling, a tortured man who was doomed to kill himself in the Bohemian Club one dark 1926 night, wrote equally tortured verse about the city he loved, but he did catch something special with "at the end of your streets are stars." William Saroyan loved San Francisco, too, but in a different way. To him it was a crazy city of wild-talking characters, most of them compulsive gamblers, and whores with hearts of gold. Mark Twain caught the frontier humor, Charles Caldwell Dobie the flavor of little North Beach restaurants, and Frank Norris the drama of everyday life behind the staid Victorian facades.

Maybe it's the great photographers who have been and are capturing San Francisco – if not its heart and soul, at least the places where they are lurking. They look at San Francisco with the most practiced and poetic of eyes, seeking the great sweep of the bridges, the incredible steepness of the streets (San Franciscans tend to take these phenomena for granted), the complicated compactness of this world-in-a-city balanced on the tip of a Peninsula, surrounded on three sides by water and always searching restless for its fourth dimension – reality.

Certainly no one recorded the death of old San Francisco with more painful felicity than Arnold Genthe, whose earthquake and fire pictures inspire disbelief (and pity) to this day and will forevermore. Through his camera, the pre-earthquake Chinatown of mandarins in their golden finery, guarded by cold-eyed men in black, comes back to instant life. You can smell the cobbled streets, hear the sizzle of ducks, follow the crooked cable car slot as it meanders up the Eastern flank of Nob Hill.

Since the age of Genthe, San Francisco has been photographed more often than a movie star, from every angle, good and bad. The degradation in the streets of the Tenderloin has not been overlooked; the record of despair is well-documented. The ticky-tackiness of certain areas of the city has drawn its share of attention – rightly – as has the bay-windowed magnificence of the "painted ladies," the Victorian houses that have at last been recognized as among our most precious legacies. This is a city that can be cold and cruel to the old and helpless; there is sadly ample photographic proof of that, too.

Of all the artists of the lens who seek to capture the San Francisco – and the Bay Area – of today, no one does it as well, I think, as Robert Cameron, who found a new way to catch and fix the elusive *persona* of this small, complicated enigma. With great style and *panache*, he rises elegantly in his helicopter, cameras at the ready, to record the changing moods and atmosphere, the peopled hills and the fog-shadowed valleys, the shifting light that makes San Francisco a photographer's dream and nightmare. He is a man of great patience, energy and dedication and his pictures reflect this. Bob Cameron will – and does – go aloft in any kind of weather, at any time, to get the shot he is after, and if it does not meet his standards, he'll do it again and again.

It has been a pleasure and education to work with him on this book. We share a love for this maddening, beguiling place, and know that we can only try, hopelessly, to find the elusive magic that holds it all together. Thanks to Bob Cameron's daring expertise, a part of that magic has been pinned down forever, like a gorgeous butterfly, between the covers of this book.

HERB CAEN

THE BAY
AND THE BRIDGES

Spectacular shot of spinnakered sailboats rounding a buoy in the midst of a race long forgotten except by the winner.

(Opposite) A beautifully composed photo at dusk of the cantilever section of the Bay Bridge plunging into Yerba Buena Island and emerging on the other side as a mighty suspension bridge. The city provides a romantic backdrop.

The *USA*, a twelve meter boat outdistances a rival in a practice race on the bay, in preparation for the America's Cup Challenge in Perth, Australia. The goal is to bring the cup back to this country, which held it from 1851 to 1983.

(Opposite) A sight near and dear to the heart of all San Franciscans — a gorgeously spinnakered sailing ship (in this case, the *Boomerang,* celebrating a St. Francis Yacht Club victory in September, 1984) flirting past an old-time "finger" pier at the base of the city's most ingratiating hill, Telegraph, with the towers of Embarcadero Center rising in the background. Showing her stern at the left is the *U.S.S. David R. Ray,* a Spruance-class destroyer. The tallish apartment building to the left of Coit Tower is 290 Lombard, built by Louise Ghirardelli of the old chocolate family. I lived there twice — happily — between marriages.

A sprightly Sunday scene with religious overtones. It's the annual blessing of the Bay's pleasure craft, promising safe voyages and trophies for all. The setting is Raccoon Strait between Belvedere Island on the left and Tiburon in the distance. Corinthian Island is on the right, marked by the handsome white clubhouse of the Corinthian Yacht Club. The San Francisco Yacht Club is at dead center but is, as always, lively.

(Opposite) A pretty shot of a pretty boat, the Hornblower Yacht Co.'s *City of San Francisco,* cruising off the Marin Headlands. The boat, a floating restaurant, was designed specifically for banquets and parties.

Dramatic pictorial evidence of Fleet Week in October 1982. That's the *U.S.S. Bremerton,* a fast attack submarine, in the foreground, and the large carrier to the right was "San Francisco's Own," the *U.S.S. Coral Sea,* then stationed in Alameda. The fireboat at the left is probably the *City of Oakland.* It's a big bay. Everybody gets into the act.

(Opposite) A Bob Cameron masterpiece: the "impossible" South tower of the Golden Gate Bridge — the one the experts said could never be anchored because of the swift currents — standing tall and secure against the Marin headlands as a freighter heads toward the setting sun and the far Pacific.

Here's Fleet Week in 1984 with the *U.S.S. Constellation,* surrounded by playful pleasure craft. The fireboat (upper left) is another "San Francisco's Own," the *Phoenix.*

It's a great day in the bay for the Navy, August 14, 1985, marking the 40th anniversary of "Peace in the Pacific." Pictured here on a calm and cloudless day are the aircraft carrier *U.S.S. Enterprise* and the battleship *U.S.S. New Jersey.*

(Opposite) After 31 years in mothballs, the *U.S.S. Missouri* has been modernized and now is rejoining the fleet. Everyone who is anyone is here on piers 30 and 32 today to partake in the recommissioning of the newest of "San Francisco's Own." The *Missouri* will be permanently stationed at Treasure Island.

Two bay landmarks unknown to many a San Franciscan who thinks he knows "everything" about the area. These are, on the left, East Brother Light Station, established by the Coast Guard in 1873, and, to the right, West Brother Island.

The station now is an inn, open to anyone willing to pay $225.00 for a quiet night in the backwaters of the bay. The bridge in the center of the photo is the Richmond-San Rafael, and San Francisco is faintly visible on the horizon.

A rare pair in a unique pose, inward bound under the Golden Gate Bridge. On the left, a replica of Sir Francis Drake's *Golden Hinde,* which sailed to San Francisco from England in 103 days on the 400th anniversary of Drake's original voyage up the California coast. On the right, the Coast Guard training barkentine, *Eagle,* on a visit from her home port of New London, Connecticut. Originally the *Horst Wessel,* named for an early hero of Nazi Germany, she was built in Hamburg in 1936 and was taken by the United States as a war prize after World War II. And a prize she is: 20,000 square feet of sail, 20 miles of rigging.

A 1934 aerial photograph of Alcatraz Island, looking neat and pristine and yet menacing as it awaits its first shipment of "incorrigible" prisoners of the gangster era, a group that would include Al Capone. Alcatraz – the word means "pelican" in Spanish – was established in the 1850s as a military prison and was famous for the first lighthouse on the Pacific Coast (1854). During its 1934-1963 heyday as a "celebrity" prison, it had a reputation for "maximum security" but several prisoners escaped, most of them never to be seen again. I once watched a strange baseball game among the prisoners of "The Rock." They were allowed one ball per game and whoever hit it over the fence – and into the bay – lost the game and the ball and a few friends.

(Opposite) Alcatraz today, warm and benign in the sun. It is now part of the Golden Gate National Recreational Area (GGNRA) and open to the public for tours of the cellblocks. There is ferry service from the mainland. Above the thrilling expanse of the Bay Bridge, a parade of clouds casting shadows on the metropolitan towers.

8-9-39) S.F. OAKLAND BRIDGE

The beginning of the San Francisco-Oakland Bay Bridge, clearly photographed on a pleasant day, August 9, 1934. In the center, of course, is Yerba Buena Island, still known among old-timers as "Goat Island," which would become the central anchorage for the great span. The wake of several ferryboats adds poignancy to this picture. As they daily passed the rising bridge, they knew their days were numbered. Note the number of ships at the finger piers at the bottom of the photo. If Harry Bridges killed the waterfront, as the propagandists would have it, there is no sign of it here.

(Opposite) The San Francisco-Oakland Bay Bridge in all its splendor, suspension, cantilever and truss. No, not a ferryboat in sight. A splendid era is long gone now.

(0102-32-I-15)(12-8-34-11:15A)(12-1000) FLEET ENTERING SAN FRANCISCO BAY

In this lively and historic photo, there is much to be seen. It was taken on December 8, 1934, as the United States Pacific Fleet – the dark-starred *U.S.S. Arizona* included – sailed into the bay, line astern, having just arrived from its permanent base in San Pedro Bay. Ferryboats stand at attention, waiting for a chance to cross the lanes; Tamalpais gazes serenely from the distance, and the towers of the as yet unfinished Golden Gate and Bay Bridges stand sentinel-straight. Note the scale of the city, the reasonable height of the skyscrapers, the open space and vistas. Just about perfect. As for the sailors, you can bet they were anxious to hit the bricks. For them, San Francisco was "Bar Harbor."

(Opposite) A 1985 Bob Cameron shot from the same angle. The towers of the city have grown but the bay and the piers are strangely empty. Item: the central anchorage of the Bay Bridge's suspension section, in the foreground, is larger then the Great Pyramid and contains more concrete than the Empire State Building.

One of the original plans for the disposition of Treasure Island after the close of the 1939-40 Golden Gate International Exposition was to have this man-made island become San Francisco's airport. Luckily, it didn't happen. The amphibious airplane in the foreground is a Sikorski S42. Three buildings, one a museum well worth a visit (the semi-circular one on the left), and a fountain are all that remain today of the fair's exhibit halls.

(Opposite) In the foreground Yerba Buena ties the Bay Bridge together and hosts the Coast Guard's Group San Francisco: the buoy tender Blackhawk and the 82 foot cutter Point Heyer provide the bay's law enforcement and search and rescue from this base. On the south side of Treasure Island the hangar-like Hall of Air Transportation is one of the remaining buildings from the Exposition.

A riveting 1946 photo of more than 100 Liberty and Victory ships, plus other military craft, at anchor in the southern reaches of the bay, awaiting decommissioning.

(Opposite) Today the Bay is quieter except during such visits as that of the *U.S.S. Missouri,* the historic and rejuvenated battleship soon to be permanently stationed here.

One of the all-time great photos of a historic moment in aviation history – the first Pan American China Clipper clearing the unfinished Golden Gate Bridge on November 22, 1935, and heading for a successful crossing of the Pacific. The adjoining photo was taken on November 22, 1985, 50 years later, when Pan Am used a 747 jetliner to fly the China Clipper route for the last time. Sadly, Pan Am no longer flies the Pacific, the ocean it opened to air travel.

(Opposite) The South tower of the Golden Gate Bridge, one of history's great feats of engineering. It is this triumph of Engineer Joseph B. Strauss that anchors "the bridge that couldn't be built."

THE CITY

In this remarkable shot, Bob Cameron captures some of the look and dilemmas of today's San Francisco — the Ferry Building tower almost hidden behind the Embarcadero Freeway, the high rises of Embarcadero Center casting long shadows and blocking once-breathtaking vistas. And yet, one must concede there is a certain power there, underlined beautifully by the camera.

(Opposite) The new look of San Francisco, pictured from another angle. The "view corridors" once held sacred by San Francisco planners obviously no longer exist in this forest of high-rises. A once perfectly balanced city has become top-heavy. The remarkable clarity and detail of this photograph tell the story all too clearly.

Lafayette Park sits atop Pacific Heights as a green oasis amid concrete, brick and glass. Up Gough, down Laguna — who stops? On a sunny afternoon sunbathers abound all tuned into a good book, a Walkman or meditation.

(Opposite) Twin Peaks, from whose heights the entire city can be seen. North Peak, to the left, rises 903.8 feet above sea level, while South Peak is 910.5 feet. To the Spaniards, the peaks were "Los Pechos de la Choca," or "The Breasts of the Indian Maiden." The red and white towers to the left are the top of a television transmitter. Straight ahead is a nice parlay: City Hall, Hartford Building, and the Trans-America Tower.

An 1865 photograph of Portsmouth Square on Kearny Street between Clay and Washington Streets, a spot that is in many ways the birthplace of San Francisco. It was July 8, 1846, that Captain John B. Montgomery anchored the *U.S.S. Portsmouth* on the then nearby waterfront, raised the American flag over the square, originally the Plaza of Yerba Buena, and claimed possession of the settlement for the United States.

Much different: Portsmouth Square today, almost lost in the midst of the largest and most bustling Asian community outside the Orient. There is now an underground garage there, plus a bridge leading across Kearny Street to a hotel that contains a Chinese Cultural Center. The hotel stands on the site of the handsome old Hall of Justice, a loss old-time San Franciscans mourn to this day.

(Opposite) The new golden roofed Stevenson Place, the twin flag-bedraped spires of the new 345 California Center and the dramatic, once controversial, Trans-America Pyramid break up the otherwise rectangular parapets of the city's skyline.

"KEY MONUMENT AND MUSIC STAND, GOLDEN GATE PARK."

"CLIFF HOUSE AND SEAL ROCKS, ADJOINING GOLDEN GATE PARK AND EXPOSITION GROUNDS."

OFFICIAL BIRD'S-EYE VIEW OF THE CALIFORNIA MIDWINTER INTERNATIONAL EXPOSITION
SAN FRANCISCO ᛒ CALIFORNIA

OFFICIALLY AUTHORIZED BY THE EXECUTIVE COMMITTEE.

A panoramic drawing of San Francisco's first great fair, the Midwinter Exposition of 1894, conceived by Michael H. deYoung, co-founder (with his brother, Charles) of the San Francisco Chronicle. The fair was staged in Golden Gate Park, which contains three survivors: the Japanese Tea Garden, the music concourse, and a vastly refurbished deYoung Museum. Originally, over 100 buildings were erected on 200 acres. The fair lasted 6 months and had a total attendance of 2,225,000.

(Opposite) The site of the Midwinter Exposition today taken from approximately the same angle. The open area center right, dominated by the tower of the deYoung Museum, was the scene of the fair. The wide, landscaped street north of the park is Park-Presidio Boulevard, slashing through the Richmond District and heading toward the Presidio and the Golden Gate Bridge.

Lombard Street in 1897, meandering down Russian Hill toward Telegraph Hill, where, on the right, is located the crenellated "castle," a resort, surmounted by a wooden-armed signal, or "telegraph," that summoned waiting ships to docking space along the waterfront.

Russian Hill today is most famous for the block between Hyde and Leavenworth Streets known as "the crookedest street in the world" because of its curlycue roadway. In the background is Yerba Buena Island in a bridgeless, but not shipless bay.

(Opposite) Lombard Street today with the eight hairpin turns of its "crookedest street" visible at the bottom. Coit Tower, the beloved landmark on Telegraph Hill, at the top of the photo, was a gift to the city in 1933 from Lillie Hitchcock Coit, a colorful woman enamored of the San Francisco Fire Department. The tower is said by some cynics to resemble the nozzle of a fire hose but that was not what the architect, Arthur Brown Jr., had in mind at all.

Photograph of SAN FRANCISCO IN RUINS FROM LAWRENCE CAPTIVE AIRSHIP

(Opposite) George Lawrence's incomparable and incredible photograph of the earthquake-and-fire ravaged city in 1906. Lawrence, who lived in Chicago, rushed to the city after learning of the disaster and brought with him 17 kites, with a panoramic camera dangling beneath them. These he flew from a ship in the bay to a height of 2000 feet to record the desolate scene. Below is a photograph of San Francisco today, taken from almost the same spot and at the same altitude.

Another kite photo (top right) by George Lawrence, taken two years later and showing, in the bay, the famous "Great White Fleet" of the United States Navy, sent around the world by President Theodore Roosevelt to "show the flag." Below right: 78 years later.

Nob Hill in the early 1920s, with the Stanford Court apartments (now a hotel); the Fairmont Hotel and the Pacific-Union Club, once the home of "Bonanza Jim" Flood, clearly visible. Still to rise are the Mark Hopkins Hotel, on the clearing to the left of the Fairmont, and Grace Cathedral, on the block beyond the Pacific Union Club. Nob Hill, so named for the "nabobs" who lived there, was once the site of the ornate mansions of the Comstock Lode and railroad millionaires, the aforementioned Flood plus Charles Crocker, Collis P. Huntington and Leland Stanford. Only the Flood house remains, extensively remodeled by architect Willis Polk.

(Opposite) Nob Hill today, a congeries of fine hotels, beautiful apartment houses and the occasional single residence. Through the years, it has changed less, perhaps, than any other San Francisco faubourg, at least in style and atmosphere. It remains one of the world's great addresses.

A 1925 photograph of an "only in San Francisco" phenomenon, Fleishhacker Pool, opened that year by the banker, Herbert Fleishhacker, as a gift to the city. Unaccountably, it was the world's largest open air salt water pool, so vast that lifeguards patrolled it in row-boats. I say unaccountable because the weather is gen-erally cold and foggy in that part of the city, and another body of water of some size, the Pacific Ocean, was close at hand. Still, it was jammed on rare sunny days. After years of disuse, Mr. Fleishhacker's white elephant was filled with earth in 1984. Some day, archeologists will puzzle over it, even as we did.

(Opposite) From the same angle, the burial of Fleishhacker Pool. Adjoining it are the grounds and buildings of the San Francisco Zoo, originally a gift from the selfsame Herbert Fleishhacker. When it opened as Fleishhacker Zoo, a child was heard out to cry, "Mommy, mommy, I want to see the fleishhackers!" The rest of the photo is dominated by the quite marvelous monotony of the Sunset District. The strip of greenery beyond is Golden Gate Park, sandwiched in from the north by the Richmond District.

Playland at the Beach - San Francisco Calif -

Playland-at-the-Beach in the 1930s, one of the world's best and most compact amusement parks, featuring a rickety roller-coaster called the Big Dipper that somehow held together till the place closed in 1972 after a 56-year run. Those of us who spent many a weekend at old Playland will never forget the Shoot the Chutes, the bumper cars, the merry-go-round (complete with gold rings) and the Fun House, with "Laughin' Sal" and an always thrilling

wooden slide three stories high. A confection called "It's It," invented at Playland, is still for sale in San Francisco and is about all that remains of this folksy, funky old rendezvous. On quiet nights, neighbors report, it is still possible to hear the shrieks of young ladies frightened out of their wits as the Big Dipper plunged yet again toward the earth, to rise safely at the last second. Sad to say, Playland has been replaced by . . .

(Opposite) Yes, yet another condominium and a supermarket ("Parking Galore!"). That's the Murphy Windmill below, recently restored by public subscription.

Fine historic shot, circa 1926, of the Pacific Heights area, showing a number of excellent houses and the first luxury apartments. The streets are, from left to right, Pacific, Broadway, Vallejo and Green. There are still empty lots, enough to make the present-day San Franciscan slaver.

(*Opposite*) This is outer Broadway today. No more vacant lots.

A rare 1928 photo of the future setting for the St. Francis Yacht Club, on the shore of the Marina, a residential district then slowly rising on land dredged from the bay for the 1915 Panama-Pacific International Exposition, a magnificent fair designed to show the world that San Francisco had recovered fully from the 1906 earthquake and fire.

(Opposite) The Marina District and the St. Francis Yacht Club today, the kind of scene that epitomizes the sometimes-Mediterranean atmosphere of San Francisco. A pastel day, marred only by the horizon-scratching skyline.

A 1930s shot of what was then a most lively part of the city – the Cliff House and Sutro Baths, the latter a remarkable pleasure dome containing a museum and a series of indoor swimming pools, their temperatures ranging from steaming hot to icy cold. It was destroyed

by fire in 1966. The Cliff House, whose finest evocation, a Victorian beauty, burned in 1894, remains pretty much as it is shown here, but the elegance is gone. Upper left is the hulk of the *S.S. Coos Bay,* which, like several other ships of the times, crashed on the rocks in a dense fog.

(Opposite) The Cliff House today, with the sad remains of Sutro Baths just beyond. Across the road from the Cliff House is Sutro Heights where a popular mayor, Adolph Sutro, once had his mansion, surrounded by gardens (still there) that were open to the public. Lower left is Seal Rocks, populated not by seals but by sea lions, but only they can tell the difference.

(032-321-15)(2-29-32-12N)(814-15000)
SAN FRANCISCO PENINSULA, CALIF.

Taken by a long-forgotten Army aerial photographer, this 1932 view from 15,000 feet shows a still bustling
port town, bridgeless but chock full of its famous streets and watery vistas, more an island than ever since.

(Opposite) A classic photo of Baghdad-by-the-Bay 1986, strutting
her gaudy stuff beneath a cloud cover worthy of Maxfield Parrish.
This is the kind of picture that brings tears to the eyes of expatriate
San Franciscans marooned in faraway places.

Hunters Point on April 23, 1932, a day not particularly famous for ideal photographic conditions. The point was named for a 49er, Robert E. Hunter, who envisioned a city there. It was William C. (Billy) Ralston, builder of the Palace Hotel, who installed the drydocks, operated first by the Union Iron Works, then by Bethlehem Steel and, during World War II, by the Navy. It is now a privately-owned ship repair facility.

(Opposite) That's the *U.S.S. Enterprise* in dry dock. In the distance, Candlestick Park, or, "The Cave of Winds."

A photo of a 1934 labor demonstration in Civic Center, dominated by San Francisco's beautiful City Hall, the work of architects Arthur Brown Jr. and John Bakewell Jr. Behind the hall, whose great Beaux Arts dome rises 11 feet seven inches higher than the Capitol in Washington, stand the then new War Memorial Opera House and Veterans Building. In the latter, the United Nations Charter was signed on June 26, 1945.

(Opposite) City Hall on a quiet, sunny day, facing the tree-lined fountain and pool of Civic Center. To the left can be seen the curving facade of Louise M. Davies Symphony Hall, while at the right is the matching curved face of a new State Building, thus bringing architectural cohesion to what is now grandly called the Performing Arts Center; it includes the new home of the San Francisco Ballet, behind the Opera House on Franklin Street.

A good shot of the South o' Market area in the mid 1930s, then named "South of the slot." The Bay Bridge has yet to be completed and the ferries still travel back and forth, as though on tracks. We are looking at a neighborhood of light industry and small businesses, most of them long since replaced in the relentless gentrification of vulnerable neighborhoods.

(Opposite) To the left, the financial district. To the right, the freeways snaking toward the Bay Bridge over what's left of South o' Market. Lots of trendy eating places now, and leather bars, discos and other artifacts of the new city. Are we having fun yet? This photo doesn't answer the question. It merely records.

The waterfront and Fisherman's Wharf in, I'd guess, the late 1930s. The WPA-built Aquatic Park building is visible, across from the Ghirardelli Chocolate Factory, and the Sanfranciscophile can pick out the Buena Vista Cafe, designed to become famous as the place where Irish Coffee became a staple of the drinking community. There are ships at the finger piers. The Depression was still on but the waterfront looks prosperous.

(Opposite) The same scene today, in glowing Cameron-color. There is still shipping, but it's mostly private, personal and for pleasure. The curving Municipal Pier is still there, and probably crowded with fishermen. Fisherman's Wharf has grown into a major tourist attraction, which is ironic since the fishing fleet itself, the reason for the entire area, has grown steadily smaller as the catches of crab and other edibles of the deep have decreased sharply.

Presidio Terrace, a semi-private enclave of handsome houses, among them the mansion of Mayor Dianne Feinstein and her husband, Richard Blum, and the marble palace occupied by Angelina Alioto, the ex-wife of a former Mayor, attorney Joseph L. Alioto.

(Opposite) Alta Plaza, one of the great, terraced open spaces, surrounded by the grand houses and apartments of Pacific Heights. There is no more desirable area to live in than this one.

The most historic building in San Francisco, and in many ways the cradle of the city, is Mission Dolores, the long, low, cross-topped building to the left of the steepled basilica. The Mission was founded by Father Francisco Palou in October of 1776, the same year that the Presidio of San Francisco was established. A historic link was forged on February 26, 1791, when Doña Concepcion Arguello, a celebrated figure in the romantic history of California, was baptized there; her father, Don Jose Arguello, was the commander of the Presidio, whose 1776 officers' club survives to this day. A statue of Father Junipero Serra, who established the California missions system, dominates the cemetery, a place of unusual interest for San Francisco history buffs. Here are buried Don Luis Antonio Arguello, first governor of Alta California under the Mexicans, and James P. Casey, lynched at the age of 27 by the Vigilance Committee ("May God Forgive My Persecutors"). Buried nearby are many pioneers whose names have become familiar street signs: Don Francisco de Haro, first mayor (alcalde) of San Francisco; Don Jose Noe, whose great ranch included Eureka Valley; Don Candelaria Valencia (Mission Dolores is located on the beautiful palm tree-lined Dolores Street at right); and Francisco Sanchez. For visitors to the city, definitely a must-see.

(Opposite) The weather in this area is some of the best in San Francisco. It is bisected by 22nd Street with Noe Valley on one side and Eureka Valley on the other. One can see that it's a short commute to downtown.

Urban renewal at its best. A far-sighted developer named Henry Adams – his name is now memorialized on a street there – took this row of abandoned warehouses, just above the freeways, and transformed them into a glittering collection of galleries, posh designers' showrooms, a vast space for public and social events, and eating places. Old San Francisco was once renowned in architectural circles for remarkably handsome brick warehouses, of which these are a prime example.

Moscone Center: more of the new San Francisco – in the foreground, a new hotel (the Air France-operated Meridien) built on what was once a saloon-studded Skid Road, Third Street. It faces a huge parking lot serving Moscone Center, named for an assassinated mayor, George Moscone, and housing a convention and display center. The empty space beyond is not the world's largest swimming pool or a reservoir, but the roof of a convention hall, built underground at great expense to appease "environmentalists." Some day – it is hoped – the concrete desert will be the site of a garden rivaling Copenhagen's Tivoli Gardens. We shall see.

(*Opposite*) Castro Street, once a quiet neighborhood thoroughfare, now the hustling bustling main street of San Francisco's gay community. At the bottom of the photo is Market Street, marching widely and gaudily from Twin Peaks to the Ferry Building.

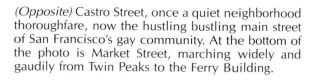

Christmas would not be complete without a visit to the Tree and Menorah in Union Square, the jewel in a ring of elegant emporia.

(Opposite) Maybe never have so many chic (and expensive) shops and stores surrounded so small an area as that of San Francisco's Union Square – slightly rounded here by the fisheye lens. The great merchandising names are all here: Saks Fifth Avenue, Neiman-Marcus, I. Magnin, Macy's and so on.

(Opposite) North Beach: The wedding cake towers of Saints Peter and Paul Church, overlooking Washington Square, the center of North Beach. Or, as the late Kevin Wallace put it, "The heart of North Beach, which is not a beach, is Washington Square, which is not square and contains a statue of Benjamin Franklin, not Washington." As I look at this lovely photo, I am reminded of another San Franciscan saying: "It is always spring in North Beach."

Coit Tower: a shot San Franciscans never tire of – Lillie Hitchcock Coit's tower, surrounded by shrubbery and lording it over Telegraph Hill, once a haunt of artists who lived in rickety little houses, now one of the highest-priced venues in town. The base of Coit Tower, "doubled" as William Powell's and Myrna Loy's home in the classic film, "The Thin Man." Beyond are empty piers, a problem the city has yet to come to grips with.

Fort Mason, once an Army installation, now part of the Golden Gate National Recreational Area, and as such, a pleasant addition to the city's life. Restaurants, theaters, galleries, studios, meeting places — in the midst of the busy city, truly an oasis. At the bottom is the apartment house known as Fontana, whose sudden appearance sparked the drive for a 40-foot height limit on the northern waterfront. Thus do we learn, the hard way.

(Opposite) The Palace of Fine Arts (foreground) is a remnant of the 1915 Panama-Pacific Exposition. Designed by Bernard Maybeck, it was built to be torn down at the fair's end but everyone thought it was too beautiful to die.

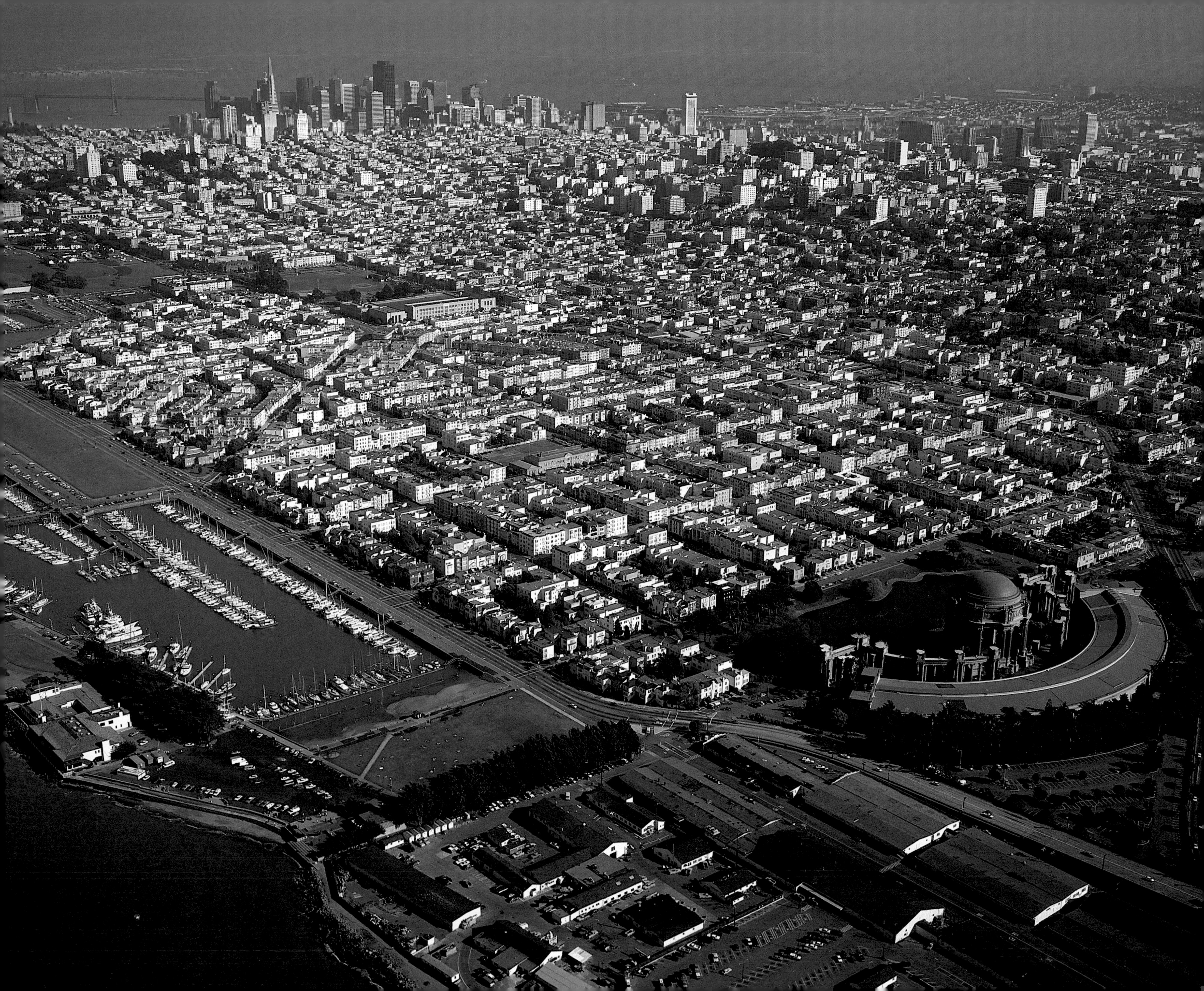

The Presidio belongs to the federal government and is shaped like a funnel ending at the toll plaza of the Golden Gate Bridge. At left is Crissy Field where Lindbergh landed his Spirit of St. Louis in 1927; it is now largely inactive save for an occasional helicopter.

"The Presidio Wall" is a phrase with much cachet among those who know their San Francisco. Some of the most delightful and coveted residences in town, several designed by Willis Polk, Maybeck and Julia Morgan, line Pacific Avenue as it runs alongside the Presidio's southern boundary.

(Opposite) Another terrific dusk shot, perhaps after the second martini. The city looks peaceful, calm, quiet when, of course, we know it is anything but. Once more on that martini, Sam.

The University of San Francisco, a top-ranked Jesuit school, its campus dominated by St. Ignatius Church.

(Opposite) Seacliff is one of San Francisco's early enclaves of beautiful homes; it surmounts a precipice of the San Francisco headlands overlooking the outer bay. Everyone here owns a telescope.

More than 100,000 souls take to the streets in the "Bay to Breakers" race each May to celebrate the circumference and run the diameter of the City. It is a record, of course, but that is only the mathematics of this new San Francisco mystique.

University of California, San Francisco, one of the world's great medical centers, a city within a city and constantly expanding. The complex is on Parnassus Heights, with the urban wilderness of Sutro Forest behind it.

(Opposite) The city at sunset, or, more enticingly, the cocktail hour. San Francisco is one of the world's great drinking cities. So many memories, so much beauty, so much to toast as the sun sets and the lights come on to blanket the hills and it's out for dinner in the city that comes to life at night.

Stern Grove, the great gift to the city by the late Simund Stern, an elder of the Levi Strauss family. The free Sunday concerts held here during the summer – opera to symphony to ballet to jazz – are among the delightful staples of the city's cultural life. Again, a great panoramic shot of San Francisco's close-coupled housing, this of some elegance.

(*Opposite*) San Francisco from the other end – the great sweep of the residential sections toward the downtown towers, with the green slash of Golden Gate Park adding its much-needed antidote to what is sometimes a sterile scene.

More fascinating facets of the city. In the foreground, the San Francisco Zoo, reaching out toward Lake Merced, a favorite fishing spot, and then on to the towers of such housing complexes as Parkmerced and Stonestown. In the foreground, the burial of Fleishhacker Pool continues.

(Opposite) Three shells and a coach work out toward the Westlake end of Lake Merced.

There are six golf courses in this picture. Most prominent is the Lakeside Course of The Olympic Club which will host the U.S. Open in 1987.

Two of San Francisco's oldest arteries, Ocean and Geneva, cross the newest, I-280 and the BART route in the Ingleside District. City College of San Francisco dominates the center of the picture and at the very bottom is where Muni's trolley cars sleep.

Here is a photo that shows strikingly the density of San Francisco middle class housing, stretching shoulder-to-shoulder for miles. The peak in the distance is the tallest in the city, 928 feet. Mt. Davidson, whose great cross is the scene of a sunrise ceremony each Easter attended by thousands of all denominations.

(Opposite) The much-maligned Candlestick Park looks better than it is. Unfortunately, it's the wrong park in the wrong place – the windiest part of the city, near Hunters Point (in the distance), but when the attractions are right, the fans will come, without a complaint. This is a 49ers-Los Angeles Rams game. The parking lots are full, the lights are on but the stadium is empty. What do you suppose that means?

THE EAST BAY

Evening commuters speed across the San Francisco Oakland Bay Bridge as the sun takes one last shot at a pink cloud.

(Opposite) Downtown Oakland in 1986, presenting an impressive sight to old-timers who have long derided it as "San Francisco's bedroom" and gloried in the signs put up by survivors of the 1906 San Francisco earthquake, "Eat, drink, and be merry for tomorrow we move to Oakland." When it appeared that Oakland had suffered little in the quake, San Franciscans quipped nastily, "There are some things even the earth can't swallow." Despite this constant and tiring bashing, and its resultant inferiority complex, Oakland has at last established its own identity, principally by developing a thriving port far better suited to containerized shipping than San Francisco's outmoded facilities. The Oakland Raiders football team — now, sadly, in Los Angeles — added to the city's confidence, as does the Oakland A's baseball team. And the comparison between Oakland's sports complex and Candlestick Park is painful for San Franciscans. Oakland is no longer a joke.

A sweeping shot of Oakland's Claremont Country Club, one of the oldest in California (1894), with a fixed membership of 750 and a waiting list four years long. Some of those waiting no doubt, made it first to the Mountain View Cemetery, to the right. The club's claim to golfing fame is that here, in 1937, Sam Snead won his first professional tournament, "The Oakland Open."

(Opposite) A Berkeley garden spot, high in the hills: the Claremont Hotel and Tennis Club, with its beautiful courts and lovely white hotel wherein "name" dance bands played for decades. In an earlier time, when the pace was slower and ferries were the only way across the bay, San Francisco couples often chose the Claremont for what they gigglingly called "illicit weekends." Such a happening is not unknown to this day, it is whispered.

BERKELEY CAL.
LOOKING EAST, FROM 1000 FT ELEVATION
FROM LAWRENCE CAPTIVE AIRSHIP
NOV 24, 1908

COPYRIGHTED 1908 BY
THE GEO. R. LAWRENCE CO.
CHICAGO, NEW YORK, WASHINGTON

A rare shot from a balloon at 1,000 feet above Berkeley in 1908. There seem
to be a lot of lots available at low prices and you would be well advised to
buy as many as you can afford plus several more.

(Opposite) Berkeley in 1985, home of the University of California and famous or infamous throughout the
country as the seat of somewhat radical – or at least unconventional – politics and of historic campus
disturbances, notably the Free Speech Movement and anti-war protests in the sixties. A sprawling city with a
beautiful residential area in the hilly region to the rear of the photo, and the birthplace of the "California
Cuisine" movement, led by Alice Waters at her Chez Panisse, a smallish restaurant that has become a shrine
among food faddists. Years ago, I coined the term "Berserkeley" to describe the offbeat activities in this lively
and idiosyncratic place. I use the word less often now but the city has lost none of its skewed vigor.

The University of California campus in 1913. Jack London had been a student here for one semester but long before this picture was made, he quit to join the oyster pirates on the bay. In fact, the whole scene is uncommonly peaceful and even somnolent.

(Opposite) The slender graceful tower in the upper center is, of course, the Campanile, the work of the noted architect and teacher, John Galen Howard. The tower dominates the present day University of California campus, with its eclectic collection of classrooms and dormitories, and its notable facilities — among them, in the foreground, Edwards Field, a track-and-field site, where the U.C. Band seems to be rehearsing; Evans Field, for baseball, and Harmon Gymnasium. Along with its generally high academic standing, the University is a center of nuclear development and research. Dr. Robert Oppenheimer was on its faculty, as was Dr. Ernest Orlando Lawrence, Nobel Prizewinner and builder of the world's first atomic bomb at the University's Los Alamos Laboratory in New Mexico. If U.C. students sometimes seem more restless and agitated than those on less volatile campuses, this could be one reason.

This exciting shot shows Oakland Airport in 1928, before it became international. No parking problems, no security checks and only a few planes out there in the middle of Nowhereville. Oakland Airport today (at the top of the adjoining photo) is a handsome and efficient place, handily close to the baseball, football and basketball complex in which Oakland takes such pardonable pride.

(Opposite) In the distance, the Oakland International Airport in 1986. Amelia Earhart took off from here in 1937 never to be heard from again. In the foreground, the Oakland Coliseum from which the Raiders took off in 1983, never to be seen again.

This sleepy-looking cow town is Walnut Creek in 1936, destined not too many years later to become a thriving city of commuters and freeways. Once again I urge you to buy some property there — at '36 prices, naturally.

(Opposite) Walnut Creek today, and now aren't you sorry you didn't buy that property? The freeway carries thousands of commuters daily to and from San Francisco, 20 miles to the west. There are some great houses here, ranging up to $600,000 or so. No longer a sleepy cow town.

Lafayette in 1936. Not too many people there to say "Lafayette, I am here!" but those who bought property soon became rich. Perhaps it is best to drop the subject.

(Opposite) Lafayette in its present state, slashed by the Interstate 680 freeway and the tracks of BART, the loosely-called Bay Area Rapid Transit, which was supposed to get people out of their cars and into state-of-the-BART trains. Proof that this is working part of the time is the huge parking lot to the left of the freeway where BART commuters park and wait for trains that often arrive, sometimes on schedule.

Another view of the curving approach to the Caldecott Tunnel, the commuter funnel. The posh area in the foregoing and to the left, is Hiller Highlands, with its country club (tennis, swimming, golf) and surrounding handsome residences, owned mainly by members. No, not a bad place to live, especially with the Tilden Regional Forest (upper left) close at hand and foot.

The road snaking across the East Bay landscape is Highway 24, a main commuter artery that leads from one bottleneck – the Bay Bridge, in the far distance – to another, the Caldecott Tunnel, at the bottom of the photo, which connects Oakland to the little world of Orinda, Walnut Creek, Lafayette, and so on. From the vantage point of Bob Cameron's helicopter, it all looks rather enchanted but do not say this to a daily commuter, cursing his way to and from work in the big city.

(Opposite) The elegant, fashionable and even snobbish enclave called Piedmont, contiguous to Oakland, but not part of it, as the Piedmontese are quick to point out. Here, the old families and the nouveaux-riches mingle in a happy miasma of self-satisfaction. To live in Piedmont is to have made it, at least in the East Bay.

In the foregound is Alameda Island, an elegant, water oriented, "thirtyish" residential community – a quiet safe-haven from the industrialized hustle-bustle of nearby Oakland since it was incorporated in 1854. Beyond is the newer Harbor Bay Isle, originally a farm and then enlarged by landfill to become a "smart" business-residential-condo modern suburb. At the top Oakland International Airport – easy access for Alameda's traveling executives.

(Opposite) In the foreground, the lush Orinda Country Club; the adjective refers to the verdant landscaping, not to the equally verdant membership.

Concord. In the foreground is Buchanan Field, which is now serviced by passenger jets and no doubt will soon glory in the name of Concord International Airport. In the rear is Mt. Diablo, tallest (3,849 feet) in the East Bay and known originally as "Sierra de los Bolbones." (The Bolbones were an Indian tribe whose warriors in 1806 defeated a Spanish party of soldiers. It was they, poor losers, who dubbed the mountain "diablo," or devil.) The Concord Pavilion, on the slopes of the mountain, houses the Concord Jazz Festival, a good one.

You are looking at Benicia and what can I tell you? The National Defense Reserve Fleet is mothballed there in the upper bay, ready for any emergency, such as a counter-attack by Grenada. The town itself is fairly colorful, with a decent collection of bars and hearty eating places.

(Opposite) A sight familiar if indefinable to most airline passengers approaching San Francisco from the east. This is the San Pablo reservoir in the East Bay. Far to the west can be seen, faintly, the Golden Gate Bridge.

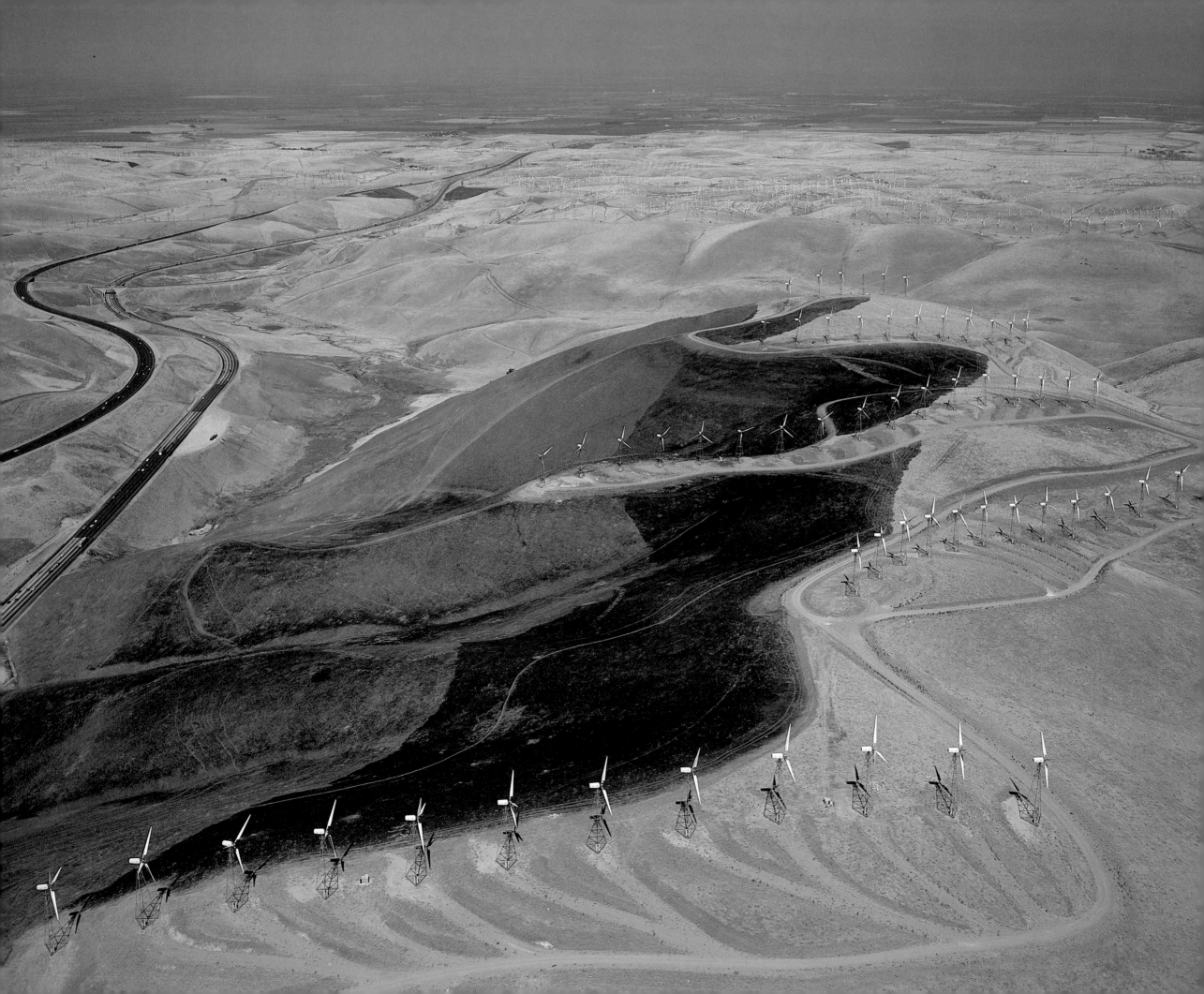

You may now say you've seen a "tank farm." These colorfully painted gasoline storage facilities dot Point San Pablo, with the Bay Bridge shining in the distance. Adjoining an even more panoramic view of tank farms, with Point Richmond, a yacht club, and one big sucker of a gas storage tank. Not shown is one of the few good eating places in the area, historic Hotel Mac.

(Opposite) Dramatic Altamont Pass and its "windmill farm," generating electricity in the most expensive way possible, in the name of "investment tax credit," and preparing for the next energy crisis. "They're not wind farms, they're tax farms," says Congressman Fortney H. (Pete) Stark, whose district includes Altamont.

Livermore is world famous – and, in some leftish circles, infamous – as the home of the Lawrence Livermore National Laboratory, managed by the University of California for the U.S. Department of Energy. You may be sure that "Star Wars" research is going on there at this very minute, as are most things nuclear in the wonderful world of warfare.

(Opposite) Yes, it is a balloon race, and one commemorating the 100th anniversary of the Wente and Concannon Wineries, which may account for the odd inclination of some of the balloons still on the ground. This exciting scene is taking place in Livermore, once famous as the birthplace of heavyweight boxer Max Baer, known as "The Livermore Butcher Boy" (he was finally butchered by Joe Louis).

THE SOUTH BAY

A dramatic shot of Highway 1, slashing through the hills and cliffs just south of San Francisco. It looks dangerous and is, being prone to slides and a touch of vertigo among sensitive travelers. Here is an unspoiled beach between Pacifica and Montara.

(Opposite) Another sight to be seen along ever fascinating Highway 1 – the beach at Año Nuevo where the elephant seals come to mate, procreate, and cogitate. Voyeurs gather at upper right to ogle.

Bay Meadows Race track in San Mateo, a folksy place.
No horses are to be seen, especially the one I bet on.

(Opposite) The Super Bowl of January, 1985, played at Stanford Stadium, with close to 94,000 people cheering on the San Francisco 49ers, who soundly defeated the Miami Dolphins. Like most Super Bowls, it was an exciting event that easily compensated for a dull football game.

We presume that George Lawrence took this aerial picture of 1906 San Jose from the same 17 kites he used to shoot the earthquake and fire pictures of San Francisco a few days earlier.

(Opposite) San Jose today, a large and growing metropolis that one day soon will surpass San Francisco in population, if not in personality, charm and reputation. To cynical San Franciscans, it is "Los Angeles North," or "The next 51 exits on the freeway." Still, there is power and ambition there, plus an excellent, Pulitzer Prize winning newspaper, the *San Jose Mercury News*. Now, the fourth largest city in California, with 700,000 residents, it will eventually rise to third and perhaps even second.

STANFORD UNIVERSITY CAMPUS *from the air.* Crandall's, Palo Alto, Calif.

This early illustration, dating back to around 1912, shows the famous Palm Drive entryway laid out by the famous Frederick Law Olmsted, creator of New York's Central Park. The architecture of the original buildings, made of sandstone, is in the "California Mission" style, with Romanesque touches in its arches.

A 1936 shot of Palo Alto, at the top, and, below and to the right, Stanford. Yes, Leland Stanford Junior University, founded in 1885 on 8200 acres by Leland Stanford and his wife Jane as a memorial to their 15-year-old son, who had died the year before. It was located on ranchland, hence the university's long-standing nickname of "The Farm." Or, more recently, "The Harvard of the West" or the West's only Ivy League school. The first class, enrolled in 1891, included Herbert Hoover among its 559 students. In 1936, it was a quiet campus of about 5000 students, with the enrollment of women limited to 500, a happy situation (for the women) that lasted 50 years. Then came equality.

(Opposite) A more recent shot of the beautiful Stanford campus, dominated by the 285-foot Hoover Tower, the school's answer to rival University of California's Campanile. The tower houses the Hoover Institution, a "think tank" that has played an important role in the administration of President Ronald Reagan. The university's enrollment today is around 12,000, and its tuition — at more than $15,000 a year — is among the highest in the country. The great white satellite dish in the foreground is part of the school's emphasis on scientific research; its facilities include the two-mile-long Linear Accelerator, an atomic energy center.

Moffett Field Naval Air Station in 1932 when great dirigibles were still in vogue and a huge hangar was under construction. This is in Mountain View, adjacent to Highway 101. The field was named for Rear Admiral William A. Moffett, who died in the crash of the dirigible Akron in 1933.

(Opposite) Moffett Field today, the home of the Ames Research Center of NASA — the National Aeronautics and Space Administration — and an important base for research and anti-submarine patrols.

San Francisco airport in the early stages of construction, sometime in the 1930s (it should be noted the airport has not been finished to this day). Originally it was known as Mills Field, in honor of the Mills estate that once occupied the land. After the 1939-1940 exposition in San Francisco Bay, the city planned to use the site, man-made Treasure Island, as the municipal airport, but then came Pearl Harbor and the Navy took over. Just as well. Can you imagine landing that close to the Bay Bridge in a dense fog?

(Opposite) San Francisco International Unfinished Airport today, fifth busiest in the country. The traffic goes 'round and 'round its circular shape, now and then dipping into the vast central garage from which many poor souls never emerge. An exciting place in many ways.

What is there to say about Mountain View in 1936 except that it was bound to grow
and it did? These dear little orchards are long gone but the blimp hangar at Moffett
Field is still part of the horizon.

(Opposite) Sunnyvale and Mountain View today, a far cry from their bucolic
beginnings but nevertheless, still a beautiful and liveable place – and one long
commute to San Francisco.

A 1937 panoramic photo of South San Francisco – then definitely "The Industrial City"
– and, further south, San Mateo. Once again, I urge you to snap up a few parcels of land.

(Opposite) South San Francisco again, de-industrialized, looking down U.S.
101, the Bayshore Freeway, toward San Bruno, and, at upper right, San Francisco
International Airport.

We are now south of San Francisco, looking at the southern slopes of San Bruno and Daly City. At the bottom of the photo is the beginning of Colma, the end of the line for thousands. Colma is a city of the dead — thousands upon thousands interred in cemeteries tended by a few hundred residents.

(Opposite) Hillsborough, one of the richest communities in the country, a semi-private preserve (no sidewalks) less than 30 minutes south of San Francisco. Here live most of the city's most powerful families, and here is the home of the Burlingame Country Club, where some of that power is exercised in the running of the city. It is all done with great taste, skill and subtlety. "Showiness" is frowned on in Hillsborough.

This is Half Moon Bay (actually Princeton, El Granada and Miramar too), one of the delightful landmarks along State Highway 1, which snakes along almost the entire length of California coastline. It is about 25 miles south of San Francisco, and a good place to stop for fresh sea food.

(Opposite) Another striking shot of Highway 1 shoreline south of San Francisco, clearly showing the caves and inlets that were said to be used extensively by rum-runners in the days of Prohibition. By any standards, one of the world's most spectacular drives.

One view of world-famous "Silicon Valley," with Apple Computers' headquarters in the foreground. Here in this complex of buildings is the culmination of the success story of the decade. Steve Jobs and Steve Wozniak found a pot of gold as they took a bite out of their rainbowed Apple.

(Opposite) The Georgian-style mansion and English gardens of Filoli in Woodside, San Mateo County, out toward San Francisco's Crystal Springs Reservoir. This lovely estate, familiar to television watchers as the setting for "Dynasty," was built in 1915 by the mining mogul, William Bowers Bourn, and bought by William P. Roth, of the Matson Shipping family in 1936. The word "Filoli" was coined by Mr. Bourn to mean "Fight, Love, Live," but Mr. Roth changed it to "Fidelity, Love, Life." Now the property of the National Trust for Historic Preservation, Filoli is open to the public Tuesday through Saturday by reservation only (phone Friends of Filoli, Woodside).

Another historic Silicon Valley success — Hewlett-Packard, founded by two Stanford graduates, Dave Packard and Bill Hewlett, in the garage behind Packard's rented house in Palo Alto in 1938. Packard, with a fortune estimated at 1.8 billion, is reputedly the richest man in the Bay Area, followed by Hewlett with $920 million. In third place, but definitely not out of the money: Gordon Getty of San Francisco.

(Opposite) In the foreground, the Syntex Corporation plant in Palo Alto, where "The Pill" was born. On the other side of the Foothill Expressway stands the Palo Alto Veterans Administration Medical Center.

THE NORTH BAY

The general term "North Bay" encompasses Marin, Sonoma, and Napa Counties and does not just stop at the other side of the Golden Gate Bridge. It is a relatively short drive to this sylvan-pristine setting of Jenner at the mouth of the Russian River.

(Opposite) Fluffy fingers of fog begin to clear the Bolinas Ridge above Stinson Beach. In an hour or so, after Muir Woods and Mill Valley have been blanketed, Sausalito and Belvedere will be socked-in.

Believe it or not, a December day in Belvedere. We are looking at the San Francisco Yacht Club (left center), flanked by comfortable houses and landscaped beauty. To the rear is Belvedere lagoon, with its waterside houses, small boats at ready. It is hard to imagine a more pleasant place to live.

(Opposite) This is the view, from the slopes of Mt. Tamalpais, that causes most motorists to pull over to the side of the road, the better to drink in its magnificence. In the right foreground is Richardson Bay, in the center is wooded Belvedere Island and just to the left, Angel Island. San Francisco and the East Bay shine in the distance. This is one of the undeniable charms of the Bay Area, this easy proximity of city and country – from metropolis to meadowland in minutes.

The lively commuter city of San Rafael, with its major tourist attraction, the Marin Civic Center (lower left), designed in pure fantasy by architect Frank Lloyd Wright. It is striking, it is famous, and it works.

(Opposite) The crooked bridge lurching across the bay at the top of this photo connects San Rafael and Richmond. Just to the right, on the Marin side, is the state penitentiary of San Quentin, home of "the fireless cooker," as prisoners call the gas chamber where Caryl Chessman was executed in 1960. In the far distance: Mt. Diablo. In the foreground: San Rafael Creek and lovely tree-shaded houses.

A fine, rare shot of Mt. Tamalpais circa 1900, showing the famous "Crookedest railroad in the world" running between the peak and Mill Valley. If you look closely at the celebrated "double bowknot" executed by the builders of this remarkable railway, you will see an engine pushing two cars up the grade. It was possible to descend by gravity, a sometimes hair-raising ride. In 1910, the mountain was crowded with people watching for Halley's Comet.

The view today from Mt. Tamalpais, affording striking evidence of the remarkable growth of this Marin County area. Richardson Bay in the foreground, Angel Island in the center of the bay, the entire spectacle quite overpowering, especially on a clear night.

(Opposite) Sausalito (the name means "willow grove" in Spanish and was originally Saucelito) was once a quiet fishing village and haven for artists, dreamers and bohemians. The Golden Gate Bridge and World War II changed all that, and today the once sleepy village is all hustle and bustle, geared to tourism in all forms. Once away from the main drag, however, there is abundant beauty amid the winding roads, rich foliage and pretty houses with extravagant bay views.

Off the Marin shores, the enchanted island of Belvedere in 1936, a quiet place where retired sea captains built their houses with a commanding view of the bay and city. To the right is tiny Tiburon and in the center is Corinthian Isle, with its white-columned yacht club.

(Opposite) Yes, Belvedere has grown. So has the San Francisco Yacht Club, off its eastern flank. A lagoon has been built to the rear, rimmed with predictably expensive houses, and Tiburon grows and grows. Despite all this "progress," it is still a charming area and great boating country.

The Veterans Hospital at Yountville, Napa County, a small town noted for a series of small and quite good restaurants. In the background is Domaine Chandon, owned by the Moet & Chandon family of France, where a restaurant serves excellent food. The Napa Valley stretching up to Mount St. Helena beyond.

Trefethen Vineyards, another highly-regarded producer, was founded in 1886 by James and George Goodman and purchased in 1968 by Gene Trefethen Jr., a retired Kaiser executive who has scored a second success.

(Opposite) The baronial estate of George Lucas, the multimillionaire movie-maker and brilliant creator of special effects. The centerpiece is the large neo-Victorian main house with its porches and gables, a romantic effusion far removed from the hard technical edge of his futuristic films of "a world that existed long ago." This spread is located "somewhere" in Marin.

A Napa Valley beauty spot — Lake Hennessey, formed by the building of Conn Dam in the hills above Rutherford. Catch yourself a fish to go with the amusing little white.

One of the jewels of the Napa Valley — the vineyards of Beaulieu, founded in 1900 by Georges de Latour, a name long famous in the French wine lands of Bordeaux and Burgundy. All bottles of Beaulieu, labeled "Georges de Latour Private Reserve" are highly prized. The chairman is Legh F. Knowles Jr., a jolly fellow who played trumpet in the Glenn Miller Band during its heyday — and who deplores "wine snobbism."

(Opposite) The very model of a major modern winery. This is Mondavi, the big and handsome "baby" of Robert Mondavi, the uncrowned king of Napa Valley. Along with producing wines of consistent quality, he and his energetic wife, Margrit, stage a highly popular summer music festival and cooking courses featuring the great chefs of France. They live on a nearby hilltop in a striking modern house with vast rooms and a large indoor swimming pool. Dry wines, a sweet life.

Still in Napa Valley and in no hurry to leave. To the right in this photo: Rutherford Hills Winery. And to the left, Claude Rouas' beautiful resort and three-star restaurant, Auberge du Soleil, with its John C. Walker-designed dining rooms (the dark, peaked buildings) and villas. Rates are predictably high.

(Opposite) This is Inglenook, about as neat, tidy and flourishing as a vineyard can get. Inglenook was founded by a Finnish sea captain, Gustave Niebaum, in 1879 and only 10 years later, his wines were winning prizes at the Paris Exposition.

To the left is the Beringer Bros. Winery, one of the oldest in the valley with "coolie-built caves," and to the right, Charles Krug, run with great success by Robert Mondavi's brother, Peter, and his sons.

(Opposite) Spring Mountain Winery in Napa Valley, familiar to television viewers as "Falcon Crest." Owner Mike Robbins' Victorian mansion (center) dates back to 1885.

Sterling, one of the newer and more striking of the valley's great vineyards. The architectural style is "Mediterranean monastery," with white walls, straight lines and rounded belfries. The bell tower contains antique English bells. The winery was opened to the public in 1973 and has been a prime attraction ever since.

(Opposite) In Napa County, the Newton Winery, one of the multitude of newer wineries, with its beautifully terraced vineyards. It is owned and operated by Peter and SuHua Newton.

The spectacular little world of Tom and Sally Jordan, whose Jordan wines (Cabernet and Chardonnay) have captivated the market since their introduction only a few years ago. The convivial couple's chateau, where they entertain frequently and lavishly, is at the upper right of the winery. This, by the way, is Alexander Valley, just north of Napa Valley.

The Geysers, 72 miles north of San Francisco in the Mayacamas Mountains of Sonoma County. Here, in 1960, the Pacific Gas and Electric Company built a geothermal power plant, providing low-cost energy for about 1.5 million homes.

This vineyard is about as far west as they get in Sonoma County.

(Opposite) Sonoma county's Russian River "winds somewhere safe to sea" — in this case, the Pacific Ocean.